Wilma
Mankiller

by Linda Lowery
illustrations by Janice Lee Porter

 M Millbrook Press/Minneapolis

I wish to thank Marsha Harlan, Norma Harvey, and Matt Manos for their help and hospitality when I visited the Cherokee Nation in Tahlequah, Oklahoma, to finish this book.—L. L.

The publisher wishes to thank Bob Annesley, Master Artist of the Five Tribes.

The photograph on page 54 appears courtesy of the Cherokee Nation, Tahlequah, Oklahoma.

Millbrook Press
A division of Lerner Publishing Group
241 First Avenue North
Minneapolis, MN 55401 U.S.A.

Website address: www.lernerbooks.com

Library of Congress Cataloging-in-Publication Data

Lowery, Linda.
  Wilma Mankiller / by Linda Lowery ; illustrations by
Janice Lee Porter.
    p. cm. — (on my own books)
  ISBN-13: 978–0–87614–880–8 (lib. bdg. : alk. paper)
  ISBN-10: 0–87614–880–1 (lib. bdg. : alk. paper)
  1. Mankiller, Wilma Pearl, 1945–   —Juvenile literature.
2. Cherokee women—Biography—Juvenile literature.
3. Cherokee women—Kings and rulers—Juvenile literature.
4. Cherokee women—Politics and government—Juvenile
literature. [1. Mankiller, Wilma Pearl, 1945–
2. Cherokee Indians—Biography. 3. Indians of North
America—Biography. 4. Women—Biography.] I. Porter,
Janice Lee, ill. II. Title. III. Series.
E99.C5M33453 1996
973'.04975'0092—dc20   95-12203
[B]

Manufactured in the United States of America
3 4 5 6 7 8 – JR – 10 09 08 07 06 05

This one's for Mike Burns & Michelle Nelson, with thanks.

—L. L.

These pictures are dedicated to Wilma Mankiller.

—J. L. P.

San Francisco, 1956

Wilma Mankiller dove under
the covers.
It was warm and safe under
the handmade quilt.
Outside, screams of wild animals
echoed off the walls.
This was Wilma's first night
in San Francisco, California,
and she was afraid.

She knew the sound of wolves.
The sound outside was not wolves.
She knew the sound of coyotes.
It was not coyotes.

When she woke up the next morning,
still yawning from too little sleep,
Wilma found out what had made
the animal screams.
It was something she had never heard
back home in Oklahoma.
It was the sound of police sirens.

San Francisco was full of things
Wilma had never seen
or heard of before.
People disappeared from her hallway
in boxes called elevators.

All night long,
flashy lights blinked on and off
outside her window.
Everything seemed strange and
frightening, so different from home.

In her mind, Wilma traveled back
to her grandfather's land on
Mankiller Flats, in Oklahoma.
Her family was happy there, living
close to other Cherokee families.
They had springwater to drink,
woods full of deer and foxes,
and a home her father had built.

But Wilma's father, Charley Mankiller,
often worried about money.
Money never went very far when there
were nine children to raise.
He wanted to give them
the best schools, the best home,
the best life he could.

When Wilma was ten,
the United States government
came up with a plan for Indian families.
They promised houses and jobs
to families who would move to cities.
At night, in their house on
Mankiller Flats, Wilma and her
brothers and sisters pressed their
ears against the bedroom door,
listening.
Their parents talked about moving.
They talked about cities like
Chicago, New York, and Detroit.
Would the schools be better
in the city?
Would life there be happier
for their children?

13

Moving sounded awful to Wilma.
Her parents, however, decided
it was a good idea.
In October 1956, the family moved
away from Mankiller Flats.

As they left, Wilma watched
very hard out the car window.
She wanted to remember everything
about the home she loved:
the colors of the birds,
the shapes of the trees,
the sounds of the animals.

In her new home, colors and shapes
and sounds were scary—and mean too.
When Wilma's new teacher called her
name in school, the class laughed.
To Cherokees, "Mankiller" was a
special title, given to someone
who protected the tribe.
To the kids in school,
it was a joke.
They teased her about how she talked.
They thought she dressed strangely.
When Wilma walked home from school,
she saw signs in shop windows.
They said, "NO DOGS, NO INDIANS."
Wilma felt as if she had moved
to the far side of the moon.

To comfort herself,
Wilma thought about home:
the hawks soaring in the sky,
the whispers of the wind
in the treetops.

She also thought of other Cherokees
who had struggled through hard times.
About 150 years ago,
many Cherokee people were forced
to move far from home.
It was a terrible journey.
It is called the Trail of Tears.
Wilma remembered the story the way
she had heard it many times
from her father and her relatives.

The Trail of Tears, 1838

Years ago, Wilma's family told her,
no Cherokees lived in Oklahoma.
Their home was the southeast.
How they loved that land!
Soft rain fell on the hills.
Apples, plums, and peaches
grew on the trees.

But white settlers wanted
the green land of the southeast.
President Andrew Jackson decided
that white settlers were more important
than the Indians who lived there.
In 1830, the president signed
the Indian Removal Act.

It was a law.

It said that all Cherokees had to
leave Georgia and Alabama,
North Carolina and South Carolina,
Tennessee and Virginia.

The Cherokees refused.

They loved their home.

So, in 1838, President Van Buren
sent in the army.
Soldiers dragged Cherokees
from their log cabins.
Soldiers loaded Cherokees
onto wagons.
Soldiers shot Cherokees
who tried to get away.

The bugles sounded.
The wagons began rolling away.
Children stood up and waved good-bye
to their mountain homes.
The Cherokees traveled 1,200 miles west,
through rain, sleet, and snow.
When wagons broke down,
some people had to walk.

In the next two years, about 17,000
Cherokees were sent west.
Four thousand died on the way.
The army left the Cherokees
on land that later became Oklahoma.
There were no houses, no churches,
and no schools.

Many mothers and fathers,
children and grandparents,
were sick from the trip.
They had nothing left
but the spirit within them.
Because of that spirit,
they survived.

Wilma had always kept the story
of the Trail of Tears in her heart.
She was the great-great-great-
granddaughter of the people
who had cried on that trail.
In San Francisco, Wilma cried too.
There, she felt lucky about
only one thing.
The Cherokee people
who had been shipped to Oklahoma
never got to go back home.
Wilma knew that one day,
she would go home again.

*Home Again
in Oklahoma, 1977*

It took her over twenty years,
but Wilma did go home.
By then, in 1977, she had
two daughters, Gina and Felicia.
She packed them up
and moved back to Mankiller Flats.

It felt wonderful
to be near Cherokee friends again.
She was happy to watch the robins
and bluebirds from her porch.
She heard the coyotes howl in the
moonlight, and she wasn't afraid.

Wilma soon got a job
with the Cherokee Nation.
Cherokees are people of two nations:
the United States and
the Cherokee Nation.
The government in Washington, D.C.,
makes all the big decisions
in the United States.
The government in Tahlequah,
Oklahoma, makes all the big decisions
in the Western Cherokee Nation.

Wilma's job was to visit Cherokee people
all over eastern Oklahoma.
Many were poor.
They had no lights in their houses
and no water.
Wilma helped them make their homes
safer and better.
One day in 1983,
Wilma was on her way to work.
She drove down a dirt road, thinking.
The chief of the Cherokee Nation
had offered her a job yesterday.
He wanted her to be his assistant
and run for deputy chief.
What an honor to be asked!
This was the second highest job
in the Cherokee Nation.

33

But Wilma was a quiet person.
To become deputy chief,
she would have to win an election.
She did not like talking to crowds.
She didn't want to be on television.
"No," she had told the chief.
Chief Swimmer had been disappointed.
"Think about it," he said.
Now, as she drove along,
she wondered if she had made
the right decision.

Suddenly, she saw something
through the oak trees.
She stopped her station wagon
and stared out the window.
There sat an old, broken-down bus.
Curtains hung in the windows.
Laundry sagged on the line.
Was this really someone's home?

Wilma got out of her car
and walked closer.
She could see
that a family lived inside.

The bus had no roof.
What happens when it rains?
she wondered.

Deep inside her,
something tugged at Wilma.
When she was a girl,
the United States government had
promised a better life for Indians
in San Francisco.
They broke their promise.
If Wilma were deputy chief,
she would have power to help change
the lives of Cherokee people.
She knew she would keep
her promises.

Stones flew as Wilma drove
to Chief Swimmer's house.
She had something to tell him.
Her time to be a leader had come.
She would run for deputy chief.

39

Wilma got right to work.

She swallowed her shyness

and talked to crowds of people.

She asked them to vote for her.

The Cherokee people had always been

grateful for Wilma's work.

They had given her warm welcomes

when she visited.

But suddenly people were unfriendly,
even angry.

Something was very wrong.

Wilma could feel it.

Soon the truth came out.

People were talking

behind Wilma's back.

"We Cherokees never had a woman
as deputy chief," they said.
"It's a job for a man," they said.
Wilma was shocked.
What a strange idea!
In history, Cherokee women
had always been treated
the same as men.

Women were medicine healers.

Women were warriors.

Women were council members.

How could anyone say only men
make good leaders?

Had the Cherokees picked up
this idea from white people?

Wilma thought so.

When white settlers came to America,
they brought new ideas with them.
Some of their ideas were good.
Some were not.
One idea was that men
were more important than women.
Wilma set out to prove
that this idea was wrong.
In her speeches, she never talked
about being a woman.
She only talked about her hopes
and dreams for the Cherokee people.
She promised to get money for houses,
hospitals, and children's centers.
She promised to help her people
make their towns better.

The trouble did not stop.
Neither did Wilma.
Someone slashed the tires
on Wilma's car.
Strangers shouted mean words
on the phone.
Someone threatened to kill her.
Everything around her was swirling
like a whirlwind.
But inside, Wilma kept still.
She reached deep down for strength.
Long ago, her people had survived
the Trail of Tears.
When she was young,
Wilma had survived San Francisco.
Wilma and the people who cried
on the trail had survived
because they knew the Cherokee Way.

You do not think about the bad things.
You think about the good.
Even if you feel you will never
make it, you move ahead.
It is called "being of good mind."
If she practiced the Cherokee Way,
Wilma knew she could survive—and
win—this election.
Finally, the Cherokee people
went to the polls to vote.
They voted for Chief Swimmer
and Wilma Mankiller.
On August 14, 1983,
Wilma became the first Cherokee woman
ever to be deputy chief.
But that was only the beginning.

When Chief Swimmer
was given a job
in Washington, D.C.,
Wilma became chief.

It was 1985 when Wilma sat down at
the chief's desk for the first time.
"You look very natural sitting
there," someone said.
People hugged Wilma.
They cried tears of happiness for her.

Wilma knew her job as chief
would be hard work.
But she was not frightened.
She felt as if all the Cherokee
people who had walked
the Trail of Tears were with her.
Their strength was her strength,
just as it had been when she was
a girl in San Francisco.
Wilma had come home to Oklahoma.
Now she was Chief Mankiller,
the first woman chief
in Cherokee history.

Afterword

Chief Mankiller was true to her word. She made sure Cherokee people had money to build homes, hospitals, and better neighborhoods. The people liked her work so much that she won two more elections, in 1987 and 1991.

Over the years, she has helped many people, especially Native American women. Now Cherokee girls know that they can grow up to be chief, if that is their dream. And people who are not Native American have a clearer idea about Indian chiefs. They are real people who go to work every day, guiding their governments.

In 1995, Wilma Mankiller decided her work as chief was over. Now she travels all over the world, telling people about Native American life. She has battled troubles of every kind, but has always found the power to survive. She says her troubles have taught her to be a leader.

She stands strong. She is a Cherokee woman.

Important Dates

1830—Indian Removal Act passed by United
    States Congress
1838—Cherokee Trail of Tears began
1839—Tahlequah (TELL-uh-kwah), Oklahoma, became
    tribal headquarters for Cherokee Nation

November 18, 1945—Wilma Pearl Mankiller born
    at Mankiller Flats, Adair County, Oklahoma
1956—Moved with family to San Francisco, California
1969—Actively supported Native American
    occupation of prison on Alcatraz Island,
    California
1977—After an unhappy marriage, moved back to
    Oklahoma with daughters Gina and Felicia
    and began working for Cherokee Nation
1979—Almost died in car accident; one year
    to recover
1981—Worked to bring water to town of Bell,
    Oklahoma
1983—Elected Deputy Chief of Cherokee Nation
1985—Became Principal Chief when Ross
    Swimmer left
1986—Married Charlie Soap
1987—Elected Principal Chief
1990—Received kidney from brother in operation
1991—Elected Principal Chief for second full term